No Excuse!

THE WORKBOOK

**Your Companion to the Book
to Help You Live
the "No Excuse!" Lifestyle**

JAY RIFENBARY

A Possibility Press Book

No Excuse!

The Workbook

Copyright © 1999 Jay Rifenbary
ISBN 0-938716-27-1

Published by
POSSIBILITY PRESS
e-mail: PossPress@aol.com

Manufactured in the United States of America

Rifenbary Training and Development Center

12 Bog Meadow Run • Saratoga Springs, NY 12866
(518) 587-6411 • (800) 724-0845 • FAX (518) 587-6417 • EMail -jnoexcuse.@aol.com

Dear Friend,

Welcome to what I have endeavored to make one of the finest success programs ever developed. *No Excuse-I'm Doing It!* is largely a culmination of the knowledge and experience I have acquired over many years, which can inspire you to achieve new heights in your personal and professional life. You can learn and begin to incorporate into your life some of the finest success principles known. Forgiveness, Self-Esteem, and Attitude are just a few of the areas that will be addressed.

The "No Excuse!" philosophy can help you unleash many of your hidden desires and talents and train you to utilize them in such a way that benefits you and those around you. The premise of *No Excuse-I'm Doing It!* centers around the concept of self-responsibility—that all of us are the decision makers and managers of our own personal lives and careers, and there is truly "No Excuse!" not to be successful.

When I adopted this philosophy, my life began to have greater meaning, purpose, and focus. It provided me the opportunity to take charge and build my life the way that I wanted it, not at the expense of others, but by helping others. It is a wonderful feeling to have a positive influence on other people and their success. Is that not true achievement in life? *No Excuse-I'm Doing It!* can provide you with the foundation and skills to develop the success you have always wanted for yourself and for the people around you.

It is a sincere pleasure to share my knowledge and experience with you, and it is my wish that the impact that this philosophy has had on my life benefits *you* even more.

Remember, there truly is "No Excuse" not to be successful in your life.

Wishing you unlimited success,

Jay Rifenbary

HOW TO BENEFIT MOST FROM THIS PROGRAM

It's important to review the material often, and refresh your mind with the ideas and exercises provided for you in this program.

You will be writing frequently. Don't try to finish the entire program at once. The more you reflect and accurately write down your thoughts, the more beneficial the program will be. Take your time and be thorough with each exercise.

Make it a priority to set aside specific time to work on the program, and be as consistent with that schedule as possible.

Share the ideas and your responses with those people who are closest to you. It may provide further knowledge, not only for yourself, but may enlighten others about you.

The affirmations included in the workbook are crucial for the reinforcement of principles and exercises. Affirmations are one of the most effective methods to retain the information and refresh your mind daily.

SUGGESTED LEARNING FORMAT

1. Read the book *No Excuse-I'm Doing It!* first; then take time to reflect on the information. If possible, have a friend read a copy as well, and share feedback with each other.

2. Prepare your mind for further in-depth involvement. Put yourself in an environment that's pleasant to work in and where you can concentrate.

3. Begin the workbook by setting aside appropriate time to do the exercises completely. Be patient!

4. Begin repeating the affirmations as often as possible. Your actions follow your thoughts.

5. Begin taking action steps to implement the "No Excuse" philosophy into your life.

6. Give yourself feedback and daily reflection on what areas you feel you improved on.

7. Share the program with others, and offer them ideas on how you believe they could benefit from it. Be creative and versatile. The program can be adapted for many individual and group needs.

CONTENTS

INTRODUCTION

The principles within *No Excuse-I'm Doing It!* are a culmination of steps that, when employed, have the power to transform mediocrity into meaningful success in your life. I will introduce to you the *THESAURUS Factor, a Staircase-of-Success* that employs some of *the* finest principles of achievement. The philosophy is designed for individuals interested in enhancing the emotional quality of their life and the lives of the people around them. Within each chapter you will be asked to participate in several exercises that will challenge your thinking and ask you to explore some of your inner feelings. As you proceed through the workbook, you will begin to discover the many wonderful attributes you possess and how living self-responsibly can transform fear of failure and rejection into an opportunity. When you incorporate the ideas presented in this workbook, you will most likely conclude that there is truly "No Excuse" not to be successful.

I was fortunate in adopting such a philosophy because I made a decision to let go of the "security" in my life and venture out on my own. As a result, I quickly needed to take on the practice of self-responsibility. However, the beauty of incorporating "No Excuse!" into your own life is that it's much easier to adopt at a more relaxed pace. It's a wonderful feeling when you understand and accept that outcomes in your life are primarily dependent on *your* actions and *your actions* alone. This realization is essential for the meaningful accomplishment of what you want to achieve in your life. Although the influences of others and the environment may contribute to your decision making process, it will still always be your decision for better or worse.

Initially, be aware that as you accept self-responsibility and a "No Excuse" philosophy, the challenge of relinquishing excuses may be difficult. Many of the habits of behavior that have become a part of your life will be put to the test. You will know that it is inappropriate to blame others or your environment for the results of your actions, personally or professionally.

This workbook is a collection of our knowledge, experience, and the influence of many great authors and speakers. I believe it will have a tremendous impact on your life and your future success.

Before we begin our journey, I would like you to realize that we are all in pretty much the same boat with respect to life's challenges. All of us face problems, discouragement, failure, personal crises, monetary difficulties, etc.; but it is how we deal with life's tribulations that, in many cases, puts us on a path of blaming and excuses or self-responsibility and independence. Living the "No Excuse" philosophy will contribute positively to putting you on the path of self-responsibility and independence and will encourage you to share in the success of yourself and others.

Welcome to the World of "No Excuse" Living ....

Part 1: Self-Responsibility

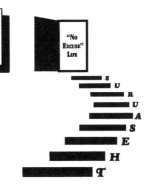

*"To become what we are, and to become what
we are capable of becoming, is the only end of life."*
— Robert Louis Stevenson

*Objective A - **To utilize the concept of self-responsibility
as the cornerstone for your success.**

*Objective B - **To eliminate the use of excuses in your
personal and professional life.**

Exercise #1 - Decision Making

Every decision you make has an impact on you and the people around you. What decisions will you be making soon (this week, month, year) that will have the most impact on your personal and professional life (e.g., buying a home, changing jobs, building a business, confronting the boss, having a child)?

#1 _____

#2 _____

#3 _____

#4 _____

#5 _____

Note: You may need to ask yourself on a regular basis, "Am I aware that I am responsible for the outcome of my decisions?"

Are you?

What would be your response if I asked you, "Do you have your own business?" Your answer could best be "yes" because everyone owns their own business; that business is YOU! You are the only one responsible for your career, and you are the only true manager of the path your career will take. When you begin to accept and practice this concept, "rev" up your engine, because you are on the runway to begin your flight to greater achievement.

Exercise #2 - Excuse Awareness

"When the going gets tough, the weak blame."
— Jay Rifenbary

Everyone, at one time or another, has used an excuse to justify a particular failure or shortcoming. However, aren't you responsible for that decision no matter what extenuating circumstances might have existed? Truly successful people take complete responsibility for the outcome of each of their decisions. Excuses cannot be a part of your growth process toward true success.

List several excuses that you or others have used recently as a reason for relinquishing responsibility or "passing-the-buck" (e.g., not enough time, too stressed-out, or my office environment).

#1 _____ #6 _____

#2 _____ #7 _____

#3 _____ #8 _____

#4 _____ #9 _____

#5 _____ #10 _____

Please classify each excuse by those that you believe you can control and those that you believe you cannot control. C - control; NC - no control (e.g. #1 time - C).

#1 _____ #2_____ #3_____ #4_____ #5_____

#6_____ #7_____ #8_____ #9_____ #10_____

Note: Examine closely the items which you marked as having no control over. Are they really uncontrollable? Is time an uncontrollable excuse, or is it one's inability to manage activities more effectively?

Notes: _____

_____

_____

Exercise #3 - Excuse Elimination

You have the ability to become excuse-free. Once you accept self-responsibility as the foundation for success, excuses become a very infrequent part of your everyday existence; they become opportunities for further personal and professional growth. For the items you have marked as something you have control (C) over, write down what you can do to eliminate these excuses (e.g., get more training, seek counseling, develop a better attitude, and open up the lines of communication).

_____

_____

_____

_____

_____

For the items you have marked as having no control (NC) over, write down what you can do to adapt your situation, behavior, and profession to them. Can you make good use of them by making them an opportunity rather than an obstacle? Be creative! Albert Einstein, Amelia Earhart, Henry Ford, Winston Churchill, Martin Luther King, Jr., and Helen Keller were all faced with what seemed like insurmountable odds, yet they all developed skills and talents to make a mark in history. Believe it or not, you too can develop skills and talents to make your own mark in history.

_____

_____

_____

_____

_____

Affirmation A - Self-responsibility is the foundation for my success. I am responsible for my success or failure based on the decisions I make. Greatness is at my door because I have the key to open it. Self-responsibility is the foundation for my success.

Affirmation B - Making excuses is a habit that shows weakness. I have the strength, talent, and desire to overcome any obstacle.

Having A Purpose Is The Key To A Successful Life

"It is difficult to say what is impossible,
for the dream of yesterday is the hope of
today and the reality of tomorrow."
Robert H. Goddard

"Some men see things as they are and say why?
I dream of things that never were and say, Why not?"
Robert F. Kennedy

Doubt can stop you in your tracks;
It can drain away desire.
Believing, on the other hand,
Can set your world afire.

When you hold the opinion that
You can reach that special dream,
You have the edge needed to make
Achieving much easier than it may seem.

Believing in your ability
Affects the way you act,
And produces an air of confidence
Which influences how others will react.

When you believe you can achieve,
And believe it with all your soul,
You possess a powerful asset.
You most likely will reach your goal.
Anonymous

"Nothing happens unless first a dream."
Carl Sandburg

"The highest reward for a person's toil is
not what they get for it, but what they
become by it."
John Ruskin

Part 2: *The Power of Purpose*

"I believe man is not in search for the meaning of life; I believe that man is in search for what it means to be alive, and if you really want to contribute to this world, teach others how to live it."

— *Joseph Campbell*

*Objective C - To create your own purpose in life.

*Objective D - To define your purpose in life.

Exercise #4 - Creating Your Purpose

"Our first journey is to find that special place for us . . . .
— *Earl Nightingale*

As esoteric as this might appear to be, defining your purpose in life is one of the most important steps in achieving overall success. Without purpose you have very little direction. With purpose you have a path to follow and a clear picture of achievement. My life changed dramatically after I took time to define my purpose. I feel it's appropriate to share it with you. "My purpose in life is to motivate others to achieve success in their lives." As a result, my thoughts and actions follow that purpose. What a difference a purpose makes. What is your purpose? The following exercise can assist you in reaching that conclusion.

Write down the following items:
Exercise #4a - What do I do well (e.g., manage, communicate, rock climb)?

#1 _____

#2 _____

#3 _____

#4 _____

#5 _____

Note: Add more lines if needed.

Exercise #4b - What do I or would I love to do (e.g., own a business, give sermons, sell computers, or help the less fortunate)?

#1 _____

#2 _____

#3 _____

#4 _____

#5 _____
Note: Add more lines if needed.

Exercise #4c - What do others like about me (e.g., my determination, my leadership ability)?

#1 _____

#2 _____

#3 _____

#4 _____

#5 _____
Note: Add more lines if needed.

Exercise #4d - What skills do I need to develop?

#1 _____

#2 _____

#3 _____

#4 _____

#5 _____
Note: Add more lines if needed.

Exercise #4e - What do others dislike about me?

#1 _____

#2 _____

#3 _____

#4 _____

#5 _____

Note: Hopefully you won't need more lines!

Exercise #5 - Defining Your Purpose

"Our aspirations are our possibilities."
    — Robert Browning

It's now essential to prioritize and combine those talents you have (Exercises 4a & 4c) with the items listed that you love to do (Exercise 4b). You'll find that when you strive for what you love and utilize the talents and strengths you possess, a definition of purpose will begin to emerge. For example: (Ex. 4a & 4c) My talents include: 1) an excellent ability to communicate, 2) advanced knowledge in the field of computers, and 3) a strong ability to manage effectively. (Ex. 4b) I would love to own my own business.

"My purpose in life is to be one of the finest computer consultants and train others in the field of computer education."

This person now has a direction to follow. Purpose is a reason for living and developing personally and professionally. Remember, like your goals, your purpose may change, but the important aspect of this entire exercise is to help you develop strong self-motivation and desire to achieve your dreams.

My top five skills are: (Ex. 4a & 4c)

#1 _____

#2 _____

#3 _____

#4 _____

#5 _____

My top two career aspirations are: (Ex. 4b)

#1 _____

#2 _____

My purpose, or one of my purposes in life, is to:

_____

_____

_____

_____

Affirmation C - My purpose in life is . . . .

Affirmation D - I have the ability, knowledge, discipline, motivation, talent, physical endurance, creativity, and monetary resources to fulfill my purpose in life.

Affirmation E - I utilize every opportunity in thought and action to support my purpose in life.

Notes: _____

_____

_____

_____

_____

_____

_____

_____

_____

Part 3: *Integrity*

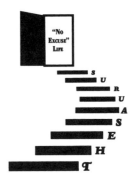

"No Excuse" Life

S
U
R
U
A
S
E
H
T

"Success is the best in you."
— Jay Rifenbary

*Objective E - **To reach an understanding that success is a matter of choice, not chance; and that whatever you define success to be in your life, as you are working toward it, you are successful.**

*Objective F - **To define the meaning of success in your life; and to realize that integrity is necessary for you to find true success.**

Exercise #6 - Society's Success

Every day we are inundated by media and people telling us what we "should" be, "should" have, "should" wear, and "should" have been. Is your definition of success based on your own expectations or on the expectations of what others think you "should be?" One of the deciding factors that determines your happiness and true success is your ability to fulfill your own needs, wants, and values. "A fish out of water is no good to itself although it may be fulfilling the appetites of many." You need to have integrity *with yourself.* Then you'll be building a solid foundation as you use your talents and skills to help others.

List several people that you or society would consider to be successful and why (e.g., Michael Jordon - famous athlete)?

#1 _____

#2 _____

#3 _____

#4 _____

#5 _____

Would you consider these people to be individuals with integrity? (If you say "no" to any one or all of them, you may want to create a new list.)

Note: Although many of the above names you listed may not have similar professions, many of them have possessed and practiced similar success principles. We all have access to these principles and the ability to develop ourselves. We all have the opportunity to act with integrity with our own needs, wants, and values as we reach out to help others.

Exercise #7 - Definitions of Success

Over the generations, society has defined for most of us what success is (money, cars, homes). However, isn't it what *we* have defined success to be that is most important? One person's success may be another's failure, yet as long as they are in the process of achieving what they define success to be, with integrity, then they're successful.

List several definitions of what you or society would consider to represent success (e.g., money, two homes, healthy family, doctoral degree, Mercedes).

#1 _____

#2 _____

#3 _____

#4 _____

#5 _____

Are all these things in integrity with *your* needs, wants, and values? If not, why?

Exercise #8 - Defining Your Success

What is *your* definition of success? Defining what you want from life is as important as defining your purpose because one supports the other. You will find that with a definition of purpose and success, based on integrity, you have begun to build the foundation for a very fulfilling future. From Exercises 6 & 7 and your own internal beliefs, compile what you believe to be your personal definition of success. For example, your definition of success may be a healthy family, fulfilling career, and owning a yacht. My personal definition of success is:

_____

_____

_____

_____

_____

Affirmation F - I have defined success as progressing toward the dreams and aspirations most important to me. My actions and thoughts are directed for their achievement. I always act with integrity based on my needs, wants, and values.

Affirmation G - Self-Responsibility, Purpose, and my Integrity-Based Personal Definition of Success are my building blocks for achievement in life. I am unstoppable!

Note: The completion of these last few pages is a major achievement. You have had an opportunity to provide yourself with the fundamental tools to build your foundation for success. Like building a home, laying the foundation is only a beginning. You are about to have the opportunity to acquire the steps that will finish the house.

Notes: _____

_____

_____

_____

_____

_____

_____

_____

_____

_____

_____

_____

_____

_____

Part 4: *The THESAURUS Factor*

"Success is a journey, not a destination."
— *Ben Sweetland*

*Objective G - **To become knowledgeable of the finest principles of success.**

*Objective H - **To utilize the principles of the *THESAURUS Factor* and incorporate them into your plan for success.**

Throughout the years, many successful people have shared their personal ideas on how to achieve success. The principles of success have their origins in many of the great books of mankind including the *Bible,* the *Koran,* the *Torah,* etc. However, more people need to apply these principles to their everyday lives.

Exercise #9 - Principles of Success

What principles of success do you consider the most important? How often do you reflect on these principles and use them in your everyday life? Granted, we can all get caught-up in the hustle-bustle of society. However, it is this hustle-bustle that some of us allow to be the major interference in the accomplishment of many of our important desires. A race car can be the fastest around the track every time on its way to victory, but if its fundamental components are not maintained (e.g., tires, oil, transmission), the car will probably not make it to the finish line. It is vital to take time to reflect on and refresh those principles that are most important to ultimate success.

List the principles that you feel are vital to achieving success (e.g., integrity, self-assurance, and discipline).

#1 _____

#2 _____

#3 _____

#4 _____

#5 _____

The *THESAURUS Factor* is a culmination of success principles that will give you the opportunity to gain the knowledge and skills to achieve a great life of significant contribution. The *THESAURUS Factor* (your *Staircase-of-Success*) will support your definitions of purpose and success and assist you in the application of self-responsibility. As mentioned earlier, the foundation for your home is: self-responsibility, purpose and integrity. How you apply each of the principles within the *THESAURUS Factor* will determine how big, fancy, or comfortable a "home" you finally create. The decision is yours.

Definition of "Thesaurus" — A place where treasure is laid up: a store house. A repository of words, of knowledge; hence, a lexicon or cyclopedia. Treasure house.

—Funk & Wagnalls Dictionary © 1978, Chicago

"Thesaurus" — your synonym for success!
Welcome to a fresh beginning. Welcome to the *THESAURUS Factor* - Your *Staircase-of-Success*.

Notes: _____

_____

_____

_____

_____

_____

_____

_____

_____

_____

_____

_____

_____

YOUR "NO EXCUSE!" WORKBOOK

Step 1: Totally Forgive

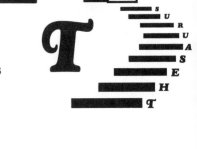

"For it is in giving that we receive."
— Saint Francis of Assisi

*Objective I - To discover the importance of forgiveness and its impact on your personal and professional development.

*Objective J - To implement forgiveness of self, others, and the environment.

As you know, success rarely happens overnight. You need to take it one step at a time. Your first step, "Totally Forgive," is an action that can help propel you along the path of success. You can only truly reach the pinnacle of success when you employ forgiveness in your personal and professional life.

It's amazing the amount of energy many of us expend as a result of the burdens we carry around of unforgiveness for ourselves and others. When you employ forgiveness, the energy you spent blaming, complaining, and whining can then be directed toward a greater outcome; achieving your dreams and goals.

Forgiveness and excuses cannot coexist with one another. One cannot blame and complain and forgive at the same time. For example, it's impossible to blame your sales manager for a lack of attention or use it as an excuse for losing a sale, and still reasonably expect to attain the #1 sales ranking in the nation. It's also meaningless to blame yourself for not getting your degree, using it as an excuse for not getting a better job, and still logically expect to become a corporate executive in a company where a degree is required. Forgive yourself and those around you for past and present failure(s), and you will find a world of opportunity awaiting you.

How do you forgive? Take the *for* from forgive and you have *give*. Whether it be through thought, word, or deed, as long as you forgive from the heart, the act is complete.

"As you sow so shall you reap." This phrase is as important and powerful as it was thousands of years ago. What you give out to those around you will eventually be returned to you. Give out honesty, integrity, and loyalty, and those same qualities will be returned to you from others.

Exercise #10 - Forgiveness Of Self

"The measure of a man is the way he bears up under misfortune."
— Plutarch

There are three fundamental areas of forgiveness that will be addressed: Forgiveness of Self, Forgiveness of Others, and Forgiveness of Environment.

Have you ever failed in life? If your answer is "No," please close the book; I wish you well. If your answer is "Yes," please congratulate yourself and join the rest of the world's inhabitants. How you deal with failure is the major factor in determining the degree of success you will achieve. Those who fail and focus on failure will surely continue to fail. Those who accept their mistake, make corrections if possible, learn from it, do not let it happen again, and move-on from it, have a far greater potential to succeed in their endeavors. Life may seem like skyscrapers and sewers. At times, we may feel as excited as though we were standing on top of a skyscraper, and other times as sad as though we were sitting at the bottom of a sewer. You can walk out of the sewers when you need to and reach the top of the next skyscraper. Remember, failure is just an event; it is not a person. It's meant to be a learning experience. What areas in your life have you failed yourself? Are you still carrying around the burdens of what you ideally could have done or what you wish you would have done? It is now time to forgive yourself and move-on. Today is the first day of the rest of your life. It is vital to reflect and learn from your past so that it contributes to rather than controls your future.

List several failure that have occurred that you feel are still getting in the way of your potential for greater success (e.g., did not get a degree, lost my first job, changed careers too soon, lost my temper with my manager or leader, quit striving).

#1 _____

#2 _____

#3 _____

#4 _____

#5 _____

Say and repeat: "I let go of past events. I start with a clean slate toward the achievement of my success.

Write: I forgive myself for the previous items because _____

_____

_____

_____

_____

_____

_____

_____

_____

_____

Exercise #11 - Forgiveness Of Others

"Forgive in life and you contribute to life."
—Jay Rifenbary

There have been many people in our lives who have influenced us both positively and negatively. Again, look at the energy you may be expending and misdirecting by carrying around the burden of ill feelings towards certain individuals. It is like Santa Claus carrying his big bag of toys around on Christmas Eve. If Santa never gives away the toys to the children and keeps putting toys in the bag, it gets heavier and heavier. Santa becomes exhausted and eventually falls to the floor. The same thing happens to us when we refuse to release the anguish we feel towards others who we have allowed to "hurt" us in the past.

Why do you forgive? Do you forgive for yourself or for the other person? You forgive for you! Whether the other person accepts your forgiveness or not becomes their responsibility because you have forgiven them. That's your responsibility. Remember, there is a difference between forgiving and forgetting. You may never forget, but you can always forgive. In fact, you need to remember so you can forgive!

My father died when I was eleven, and I carried anger and resentment around with me for many years. Also, it was a great excuse to use when life's events would "go astray." It was not too long after adopting the "No Excuse" philosophy, that I was able to forgive him and release that burden. That forgiveness in itself released a lot of energy that now can be dedicated toward developing myself, as well as helping others.

Whether it's in sales, management, marriage, friendship, athletics, or another area of your life, forgiveness can add years of happiness and vitality to your life. Who have you allowed to hurt you in the past? What business associate stabbed you in the back? What account did you lose because of the incompetence you felt of someone else? Are you still carrying grudges, such as these, around with you?

List several people who have had a negative influence on your life. Remember, by forgiving these individuals the energy which had been used to harbor anger, frustration, and resentment can now be released and redirected for the benefit of you and your future.

#1 _____

#2 _____

#3 _____

#4 _____

#5 _____

List several ways in which you could go about forgiving the individuals named above (e.g., card, letter, thought, or phone call).

#1 _____

#2 _____

#3 _____

#4 _____

#5 _____

Write: I forgive you__(name)__for the hardship and negative influence you have had on my life. I let go of any resentment towards you and things you have done. My current and future success is free of any negative influence from your past actions.

I forgive _____

I forgive _____

I forgive _____

I forgive _____

I forgive _____

Exercise #12 - Forgiveness Of Environment

"Your perception of the external will shape the internal."
— *Jay Rifenbary*

If you have ever been stuck in traffic, bogged down by a snow storm, worked in an unpleasant office environment, or felt the impact of a recession, you understand the influence your environment can have on your motivation to succeed. In all actuality however, your environment is not to be used as an excuse, and it does not control the outcome of your endeavors. Can you legitimately blame the weather for not closing a sale? Would it be appropriate to use your car as an excuse for being consistently late for appointments? Of course not! Like forgiveness of yourself and others, it is important to forgive your environment. You can then use the energy which was directed on blaming to nourish your personal and professional development.

What elements of the environment have I used regularly for excuse-making? What elements of the environment will I forgive and no longer use to avoid self-responsibility?

#1 _____

#2 _____

#3 _____

#4 _____

#5 _____

Write: I forgive my environment and no longer use it as an excuse because _____

_____

_____

_____

Affirmation H - I forgive myself for any past failures. I direct my energy towards the accomplishment of my future dreams and aspirations. I forgive myself.

Affirmation I - I forgive those who I feel have "hurt" me in some way. I realize that their past actions are not to be used as an excuse for a lack of achievement.

Affirmation J - I forgive my environment and realize that it does not control the outcome of my decisions.

Step 2: *Have Self-Esteem*

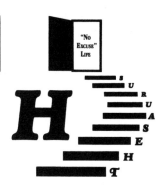

"When our self-esteem is intact we don't fear failure and rejection."

*Objective K - To understand the essential nature of self-esteem and its origin.

*Objective L - To be able to overcome the fears of failure and rejection, and take steps to enhance self-esteem.

Self-esteem is the respect we feel for ourselves. Society's influence on our self-esteem can be destructive. If you don't drive this car, wear these clothes, own this home, live in this area, or belong to this group, you are often considered unsuccessful. Remember, satisfaction in life is not satisfaction with the external, it is satisfaction with the internal. Our children face a similar plight, for they are impacted daily by the influences of peers, radio, videos, television, and perhaps by computer communications. Instill in them, that like us, they are special people with special gifts.

Exercise #13 - "Self-Esteem Perception"

What respect do I feel for myself? What qualities do I possess that make me unique and special (e.g., sense of humor, sensitivity, empathy)? Appreciate yourself! Feel happy about yourself. List several characteristics that represent the best in you.

#1 _____

#2 _____

#3 _____

#4 _____

#5 _____

You are a wonderful person! Respect yourself and believe in who and what you are. This is essential to your personal growth and achievement. Unintact self-esteem can be extremely self-destructive. Self-esteem gives you the foundation for your belief in yourself. A climber can never reach the top of Mt. Everest if he is not trained in the basics of climbing. When you disrespect yourself and therefore, limit belief in yourself, you limit your potential for success. "What I see in me, is a mirror of me; my reflection will undoubtedly be my direction."

Challenging situations are a part of everyday life. How we handle them is an indicator of our self-esteem. Remember, it's not what you are given, it's how you respond to it. It is also true that an unintact self-esteem breeds excuses and minimal acceptance of self-responsibility.

The roots of self-esteem begin during childhood. Our parents (or caretakers) have had the major influence in the development of it. Two major variables that result from how we were "parented" are the "fear of failure" and the "fear of rejection." Our parents' influence in the past is likely to still affect us today. It is the state of our self-esteem that determines how much we let the fear of rejection and failure control our lives. The more respect we have for ourselves and thus, the greater the belief we have in ourselves, the less failure and rejection interferes with our achievement of our goals and dreams.

Exercise #14 - "Fear Of Failure/Fear Of Rejection"

"Nothing in life is to be feared. It is only to be understood."
                              — Marie Curie

On a scale of 1 to 10 how would you measure your fear of failure and fear of rejection?
   Fear of Failure -   1   2   3   4   5   6   7   8   9   10   *(circle one)*
      1 - would try anything   10 - avoid all risks
   Fear of Rejection -   1   2   3   4   5   6   7   8   9   10   *(circle one)*
      1 - emotionally numb to people's comments   10 - avoid criticism at all costs

Hopefully you are not either one or ten but somewhere around the five area. Almost everyone fears failure and rejection to a degree. It only becomes harmful when it begins to dominate behavior and lifestyle.

Remember:
   "When you fear failure, you fear yourself!"
   "When you fear rejection, you fear others!"

Notes: _____

_____

_____

Exercise #15 - Reducing Fear Of Failure And Rejection

You have probably wanted to make changes in your life at one time or another. What reasons have held you back? Has the fear of failure or rejection played a role? Has the fear of failure or rejection interferred with your desire to take a chance on something you've always wanted to do (e.g., begin a new career, own your own business, go back to school, start a hobby, or confront family problems)?

List several desires or changes that you want, or have wanted to begin, but your underlying fears of failure or rejection have influenced you not to take action.

#1 _____

#2 _____

#3 _____

#4 _____

#5 _____

There are many ways to overcome these fears which relate directly to the development of intact self-esteem. For example, the more you incorporate the principles of honesty and integrity into your life, the less you will fear others' comments. The more you practice self-responsibility, the less inhibited you are likely to be to try something new. Both actions enhance your self-esteem.

With intact self-esteem comes a strong sense of security and self-confidence. As a result, fear of failure and rejection have less of an influence on your decision making process. If you truly believe in yourself and your talents, whatever you change or strive for can be a valuable investment in yourself, your career, and your family. Your continued march along the *Staircase-of-Success* can help you enhance your self-esteem, raise your sense of security, and elevate your commitment to strive for excellence in all you do.

You have already taken the first step towards enhancing your self-esteem. Your application of forgiveness will have a very positive impact on it. When you forgive yourself, others, and your environment, I believe you'll begin to feel better about who you are and what you are doing. As you begin to live a "No Excuse" lifestyle, you'll discover an even greater potential for fulfillment.

Affirmation K - I believe in myself, and my abilities. I have the self-esteem, confidence, determination, and talent to accomplish all my dreams and goals.

Affirmation L - I overcome any fear of rejection or failure. I am confident of the decisions I make for myself, my family, and at work.

Attitune-Ups

No one can ruin your day without YOUR permission.

Most people will be about as happy as they choose to be.

Adversity introduces a person to themselves.

The greatest discovery in the world is SELF DISCOVERY.

It's always too soon to quit.

People who win in life, persevere.

Always maintain your taste for success.

The point of living is to believe that the best is yet to come.

Everyone has a fair turn to be as great as they want to be.

It's useless to wait for your ship to come in unless you have already sent it out.

There is no future in any job. The future lies in the person holding the job.

Positive anything is better than negative nothing.

The most extraordinary thing a person can do is to do the best they can.

The person who feels certain of not succeeding is seldom mistaken.

There isn't any particular map to success; you need to find your own way.

Go out on a limb once in a while. That's where the fruit is.

All people smile in the same language.

*Happiness is like a kiss. In order to get any good out of it,
you need to give it to someone else.*

Happiness is a habit. Cultivate it.

Life is not about having and getting, it's about being, becoming and giving.

Be what you want others to become.

Empathy is the hand up the ladder.

*If there were no storms, where would the blessed showers
and beautiful rainbows come from?*

Author Unknown

Step 3: *Elevate Your Attitude & Enthusiasm*

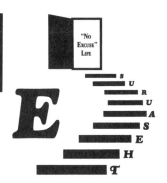

"Success is going from failure to failure without loss of enthusiasm." —Winston Churchill

*Objective M - To become aware of the impact that a negative attitude has on your personal and professional life.

*Objective N - To use perception as a key to maintaining a positive mental attitude.

How do you feel when your boss or the people you work with are "down in the dumps"? How is your productivity affected when their attitude is low? How are cooperation, communication with others, personal relationships, self-motivation, desire, perseverance, and other behavior-related activities affected by a negative attitude? Negative attitudes can be one of the most powerful and immediate factors that influences your business and personal success, if you let it. Your attitude is also an excellent indicator of whether your self-esteem is intact. When you feel wonderful about who you are, it is directly revealed to others through your attitude. Attitude is the medium by which we communicate our mental and physical well-being to others. It represents the degree of professionalism, maturity, security, self-awareness, and other attributes we possess. A correct mental attitude is crucial for achievement.

A boss with a negative attitude who is blaming and complaining usually has an immediate impact on the productivity of their employees. The end result is often discouragement, discontent, lower motivation, and a lower profit margin for the organization. You cannot afford to bring yourself or others down by a negative attitude. Life has too much potential for joy to waste time on everything that you perceive is "wrong" with it. More beneficial things are likely to happen when you get excited and have an uplifting attitude.

Attitude is your latitude and longitude in life. It's the first impression you give to others. It's your expression that determines your direction. Would you hire someone who walks into an interview with their head down and begins whining about benefits? Of course not!

As a rule, people prefer to associate with positive, enthusiastic people. When our focus is on the positive and not the negative, we can bring out the best in ourselves and others. When you and your organization focus on development, growth, and innovation, for example, the end result is likely to be beneficial to everyone concerned. I encourage you to associate with positive people rather than negative ones. It takes much less energy to complain and go with the flow than it does to set the example and take action. Your decision to be a positive enthusiast will take effort, yet so does a manager's decision to promote someone! It's worth it.

Exercise #16 - Attitude Awareness

We can all have a negative attitude at times; that's human nature. As with any habit, it's the consistency of our actions that determines how strong a habit we develop. Like smoking, drinking, consuming caffeine, and overeating, a consistent negative attitude can become a dangerous habit, with debilitating effects.

List several events in your life which have occurred where you feel a negative attitude has had an impact on your personal and professional growth. Note: This could be a result of your actions or someone else's (e.g., going into your last sales call thinking you won't close the sale and coming out without the sale; going on a vacation focusing on the expense and hassles and as a result, you're unhappy most of the time there).

#1 _____

#2 _____

#3 _____

#4 _____

#5 _____

Ask yourself: Was the negativity beneficial in any way? What areas in your daily life would benefit most from a positive attitude (e.g., home, work)?

#1 _____

#2 _____

#3 _____

#4 _____

#5 _____

Exercise #17 - "Attitude Adjustment"

You can deal with an employee's negative attitude in two ways: retrain the employee or release the employee. If you are a manager, you may be the best person to weigh the cost effectiveness of either decision. However, when the negative attitude of one affects the positive attitude of others, then a decision needs to be made.

If you are an employee, it's your decision whether you'll associate or disassociate with people who consistently have a negative attitude. Be different by being positive and enthusiastic!

Changing your attitude is a result of changing your perception. A "Beware of Dog" sign is perceived differently on someone's front lawn than it is when hung on your boss's door (most of the time). When you practice changing perceptions, what was once considered a negative can turn into a positive. A lost sale, although disappointing, can be looked at as an opportunity to avoid making the same mistake. Granted it requires effort to change your perception. However, the way we think can either create problems or negate them.

Give several examples of situations that would typically be considered as negative, yet by changing your perception, could be turned around into positive opportunities. State why (e.g., a recession — a chance to be creative and set yourself and your business apart from the rest; unhappiness — a chance to find out the reasons why).

#1 _____

#2 _____

#3 _____

#4 _____

#5 _____

Society has impacted our perceptions in many areas (e.g., what success is, what marriage "should" be, and what life "should" be). Our perceptions are based on our personal history, beliefs, and value structure. When society's perceptions conflict with our perceptions, frustration and negativity may result. For example, society's perception of your self worth is money, and you are not making any, are you then worthless? Your acceptance of society's belief can have a deteriorating effect on your attitude and enthusiasm.

How you perceive and what you believe help structure what you achieve. Attitude, as Earl Nightingale noted, is the "Magic Word." It can produce magical results at home, work, and play. Maintain a positive attitude with others, and you can help to uplift others as well as yourself. Norman Vincent Peale once stated, "enthusiasm makes the difference!"

Even in this short period of time climbing the *Staircase,* you have accomplished a tremendous challenge, and I congratulate you. With self-responsibility, integrity and purpose, you have established your foundation. With totally forgive, have self-esteem, and elevate your attitude and enthusiasm, the first floor is solid and well-designed. Remember, "A smile makes everything worthwhile."

Affirmation M - I maintain a positive, enthusiastic attitude towards myself and others.

Affirmation N - My positive attitude is an example for others to follow, and it motivates me to perform with enthusiasm.

Step 4: *Sustain Self-Control*

"The greatest potential for control tends to exist at the point where action takes place."

— *Louis A. Allen*

*Objective O - To be aware of the importance of self-control, and its impact on everything that you do.

*Objective P - To develop self-control in thought, word, and deed.

What happens when someone loses control? How do you respond? How does it affect your productivity, attitude, motivation, and work efficiency? In a crisis situation, do you focus on the crisis or the person who caused it? Do you respond with emotion or logic?

Maintaining consistent self-control in everything that you do is critical for success. It's a measure of the quality of your leadership skills and professionalism. A loss of self-control can seriously change a workable situation into what seems like a lost cause. When anger, blame, impatience, and other destructive emotions become a part of the decision making process, damaging consequences may occur.

How do you feel when someone you work with or your manager reacts with negative emotion? In most cases, their display of a negative emotion affects how you communicate with that person in the future. If anger is their consistent response to challenges, then you are more likely to withhold information to avoid the potential for that anger. Self-control can affect the quality and quantity of ongoing communication in the office and at home. When it is time to make a decision or respond to a crisis, maintain a level of professionalism and consistency in your actions. This will assist others in their actions and reactions to you. Granted, there are times where a change in behavior can be beneficial, as long as it's not at the expense of others.

While in the service and in corporate life, I witnessed many individuals ruin their careers because they lost self-control. They may have been an excellent platoon leader, salesperson, or manager. However, because they lost control, for example, at a social event, they lost respect from their peers and superiors alike. As a result, their potential for promotion and greater responsibilities was negatively affected.

Exercise #18 - Factors of Self-Control

There are many factors which may influence our ability to maintain self-control (e.g., family, traffic jams, deadlines, and other people) if we let them. What factors this past week or month have tested your ability to maintain self-control?

#1 _____

#2 _____

#3 _____

#4 _____

#5 _____

Did any of these items influence you to lose control? If so, do you believe your loss of self-control affected the people around you? Did it have a negative impact at work or home? State how and why (e.g., missed deadline or lost temper with someone) this impacted on their attitude(s).

#1 _____

#2 _____

#3 _____

#4 _____

#5 _____

Remember, how you respond to a situation determines whether the outcome is positive or negative. When emotion takes precedence over clear thinking, opportunities for failure arise, both personally and professionally.

Of all the areas in your life that you are involved in, where, ideally, could you have the most control? <u>AT HOME</u>!

At work, you are probably nice to people all day, right? You are likely to be courteous, patient, kind, and sympathetic. You may maintain self-control for people you don't even know, and even for those who are discourteous to you. However, when you go home, the self-control you maintained at work may suddenly become less important. Your children or spouse may do or say something that you don't like and "boom" you may lose control. Your family are the people for whom you could best maintain the most self-control. Home is not meant to be the place to release our frustrations and anger. It is hard to justify maintaining self-control for a stranger and not for the ones we love. Ask yourself, "Have I put the same priority on self-control at home as I do at work?"

Patience is the foundation for maintaining self-control. The old cliches of "haste makes waste" and "patience is a virtue" are more important today than ever before. It is one thing to want it all immediately; it is something else to act that way. True success does not happen overnight. Remember, "get rich quick" schemes are just that, they are quick and never last. It was the "little pig" that built his house with bricks that protected him from the big, bad wolf. His patience won out.

Exercise #19 - "Patience is a Virtue"

Have you ever really wanted something, yet because it didn't happen quickly enough, you stopped working towards it and now regret that you gave up? List several events where a lack of patience had a negative result (e.g., giving up on a worthwhile relationship without giving it a chance, closing a business that you know had the potential to be successful).

#1 _____

#2 _____

#3 _____

#4 _____

#5 _____

If you still want those items above, do you believe you can still achieve them (or something similar)? It's likely that you can! Incorporating self-control into your professional and personal life can provide greater harmony and peace of mind for you and your family. Take the time to reflect and examine those areas in your life where your application of self-control is needed or where it can be improved. Greater responsibility, professionalism, leadership qualities, a happier family life, and a larger income can be some of your rewards when you strive for success with patience and self-control.

Affirmation O - I maintain self-control in everything I do, in thought, word, and deed.

Affirmation P - True success takes time, and I possess the patience and determination to see all my endeavors through to their completion.

Notes: _____

_____

_____

Step 5: *Always Be Honest*

"You cannot do wrong without suffering wrong."
— *Ralph Waldo Emerson*

*Objective Q - To realize above all else, that honesty is the principle to cherish the most.

5 - *Always Be Honest*

Without honesty and trust there is no true personal success. A person may have all the riches in the world, but if he achieved them dishonestly, then his achievements are meaningless. What you give out to others will be returned by the recipient or someone else. When you are honest with yourself and others, they are more likely to be honest with you.

Of all the attributes of my business, the ones I value the most are honesty and integrity. I find that when people can trust what I say and do, they are likely to continue doing business with me and encourage others to do the same. When a person or business jeopardizes their integrity, the potential for problems and failure rises dramatically.

At my alma mater, the United States Military Academy, West Point, N.Y., the motto, "Duty" "Honor" "Country" and the honor code, "A cadet will not lie, cheat, steal, or tolerate those who do," are held in the highest esteem. These moral codes encourage fairness and a feeling of self-esteem for those who adhere to them. Honesty helps you have greater respect for and acceptance of yourself both in success and failure. Remember, it is better to be remembered for what we gave to life than what we took from life. Nice guys don't usually finish last!

*The one universal question that we all ask of one another is, "Can I trust you?" You ask that of me; I ask that of you. Your parents asked that of you; you asked that of your parents. Your clients ask that of you; you ask that of your clients. That is why maintaining honesty and integrity in everything you do is vital for the accomplishment of your dreams and goals. Honesty is a reflection of what you stand for and who you are. How can you believe in yourself, respect yourself, and feel happy with yourself if a lack of honesty prevails in your personal and professional life? It is impossible to truly achieve if you deceive.

Notes: _____

_____

_____

_____

* This idea was inspired by Lou Holtz in his book, *The Fighting Spirit* © 1989, New York

Exercise #20 - Honesty is the Best Policy

What areas in life do you feel honesty is the most important principle (e.g., with my children, spouse, or work).

#1 _____

#2 _____

#3 _____

#4 _____

#5 _____

It's amazing how dishonesty always returns to the people who are dishonest. There have been many individuals who were initially considered great, until dishonesty returned to haunt them. The greatest failures in life have been moral failures not business failures. The names of several individuals may come to mind, whose power and fame tumbled because of a moral failure.

List several people who you feel have destroyed themselves because of a moral failure or by being dishonest. Have you witnessed this in your own local area or business community?

#1 _____

#2 _____

#3 _____

#4 _____

#5 _____

Hold the values of honesty and integrity close to your heart, for they will help you have the strength and character to overcome difficulties.

Notes: _____

_____

_____

Step 5A: *Always Dream & Set Goals*

"The big thing is that you know what you want."
— *Earl Nightingale*

*Objective R - To develop and write down specific dreams and goals for your personal and professional life.

In exercises #7 and #8 you had an opportunity to define what success means to you. What is your definition of success? Your answers are the framework for your goals. Goals are your definition of success. That is why, without goals, you have no direction or path to follow. Mark Twain once said, "Without dreams you may still exist, but you've ceased to really live."

Of all the steps to success, setting goals is the most tangible. You can actually work with goals because you have the opportunity to write them down, review them, see them, update them, and adapt them to your needs and wants. Unfortunately, many people plan what they will watch on T.V. at night more carefully than they plan their careers and personal lives. The principles of success support your achievement of your goals and therefore, your definition of success. If you have a goal of showing an example of leadership for your employees, your attitude and self-esteem are critical. If you have the goal of enhancing your personal relationships with your family, forgiveness is essential. If you have the goal of confronting your superior about an issue, self-control will be needed. Every day there's a goal to achieve. Every day, as well, other principles influence the accomplishment of those goals.

Goal setting can help you to avoid the "hamster syndrome." Have you ever seen a caged hamster running all day in its little wheel? By the end of the day the hamster is exhausted, its eyes are bulged out, it's hungry, and yet, it is at the same place where it started. Have you ever felt like that at the end of the day? If you have, you are not alone.

Exercise #21 - Writing Your Goals

One key of goal setting is that goals need to be specific. Saying you want to be financially secure is a wish. Establishing in writing that you want to make $1,500,000 by a certain month, day, and year is a specific goal. Why is it important to write goals down? It is well known that when you write down your thoughts (e.g., goals), they are embedded into your subconscious, and as a result, support your actions. The more you reinforce your thoughts (goals) by writing them down, the more effective your actions that follow.

What are your goals? What do you want to achieve **tomorrow, next week, next month, next year?** What are several goals that you would like to accomplish in the next twelve months (e.g., be #1 salesperson, buy a new home, or achieve 120% of quota)?

#1 _____

#2 _____

#3 _____

#4 _____

What do you want to accomplish within **the next three years** (e.g., be promoted to district manager and/or start a family)?

#1 _____

#2 _____

#3 _____

#4 _____

What do you want to accomplish within **the next five years** (e.g., start my own business and/or be regional director)?

#1 _____

#2 _____

#3 _____

#4 _____

It is important to invest some time in your goals every day. We are all affected by factors that threaten to interfere with our daily schedule and "to do" lists. However, those factors are not to be used as an excuse for not achieving the goals we have set. You may need to change the target time or date of your goal completion, though.

The things we want most in life often tend to be the most difficult and may take the most time to complete. As with electricity and water, it is human nature to want to follow the path of least resistance. Real success is rarely quick or easy. Develop a dream and a passion for what you want to do with your life, and go do it. Life's too short not to do so. Having a big dream will help you to plan through any obstacle. Make your dream bigger than the task, and this will help do what you need to do to make it come true.

Here's a very effective method that you can use to keep your priorities in order. The "Goal Prioritizing Grid."

URGENT

Priority #1
(Day-to-day routines)

_____

_____

_____

_____

Priority #3
(Interruptions-Reactive)

_____

_____

_____

_____

IMPORTANT_____**NOT IMPORTANT**

Priority #2
(Goals-Proactive)

_____

_____

_____

_____

Priority #4
(Don't Bother)

_____

_____

_____

_____

NOT URGENT

THE GOAL PRIORITIZING GRID

Priority 1 - important & urgent are the daily items that *definitely need* be accomplished. Those are the routine tasks that support the daily operation and existence of the organization or individual (e.g., daily reports, bills, eating, and sleeping).

Priority 2 - important & not urgent is the crucial block for long term success because your long term goals would be placed here.

Priority 3 - urgent & not important are the items that we tend to give a sense of urgency, based on our comfort zone (what we are used to). Simple things like social phone calls and rearranging your desk go here.

Priority 4 - not urgent & not important are those items that take care of themselves. Don't spend any excess time on them, for they do nothing to contribute to your growth (e.g., watching a TV show that doesn't inform or educate you about something important to your future).

The major factor that inhibits our progression to our goals is the conflict between Priority 2 and Priority 3. It may seem impressive to have a "to do list" of 30 items and have 28 of them crossed out. However, if you accomplished items that were urgent yet not important, did you spend your time wisely? As Peter Drucker said, "It is often more important to do the right things than to do things right."

What is easier—rearranging your desk or starting on that sales report? Finding new clients or stopping by to see the old ones to say "hi"? Working on your relationship or giving up? Changing certain behavior patterns (e.g., drinking, smoking, eating) or making excuses why you "can't"?

Once again, if you do not accomplish what you want most, the door of excuses and complaining can swing wide open. You have the talent and can develop the desire and discipline to accomplish your goals. Realize that your achievements come mostly from directed time and effort on your part. Sure, you can receive support from others, but "tag you are it"; you are the main person responsible for these accomplishments.

Exercise #22 - Priority Setting

Take the time now to list certain items in each block of the "Grid" (e.g., 1-daily sales report, 2-#1 in the sales district, 3-clean my file cabinet, 4-opening the unimportant mail).

Examine what items in your daily environment are listed in priority 3 and ask yourself. "Do they interfere with what I have listed in Priority #2?" If they are having a detrimental impact, it is imperative to learn to skillfully manage your activities more effectively, so that you can spend the necessary time working towards the accomplishment of your goals.

With each goal, you need a plan of action. It is one thing to have goals; it is something else to take the initiative and begin implementing the tasks to accomplish them. Your decision, commitment, and focused action are the requirements needed for their achievement. It's simple.

Review your goals daily, and have them in an area where you can readily refer to them. It's a wonderful feeling when you see the results of your efforts be rewarded by the accomplishments of your goals.

Affirmation Q - I am honest and sincere in everything I say and do. I always act with honesty and integrity.

Affirmation R - I always have written goals. Goals define my success and provide me the direction to employ my talents and accomplish my dreams.

Step 6: *Upgrade Your Knowledge*

"Wisdom is meaningless until our own experience has given it meaning."

— *Bergan Evans*

*Objective S - **To commit yourself to utilizing the many resources available for enhancing your knowledge and professional and personal skills.**

Knowledge provides the catalyst for all success. Through knowledge we achieve understanding, and understanding provides the foundation for wisdom. We need to learn, to grow. Your participation in this program can help you enhance your knowledge, and provide you the opportunity for greater understanding.

All of us possess the innate potential to increase our knowledge; however, it is amazing to see the number of people who completely neglect any opportunity to become well-informed. If you want to be an excellent salesperson, manager, spouse, baker, parent, rocket scientist, or something else, the resources are available. There are books, tapes, and videos on almost any topic that you may be interested in learning. The professional with well-developed skills dedicates time and energy to continued personal and professional development. If you want to be excellent in your profession, it's essential that you devote time to studying and learning. Are you aware that the average person uses less than 32% of his or her brain power? I certainly wouldn't want to conduct business with or hire someone who used only 1%! Would you? Without knowledge or access to knowledge there is no success. Knowledge is an essential part of success.

It's also important to understand that what you learn and how knowledgeable you are is determined by you and your wants and needs. If you have a need to develop your management skills, then studying about gardening may not be necessary. Mother Theresa knew very little about nuclear physics, however, she was one of the most knowledgeable people in the world about human suffering and was recognized for her compassion to others. It is important to spend time on the resources that will contribute to the further development of your interests, skills, and your over-all career.

Notes: _____

_____

Exercise #23 - Knowledge Inventory

What was the last book you read?   When?

_____

What was the last audio tape you listened to?   When?

_____

What was the last seminar you attended or watched?   When?

_____

Did these items you listed above contribute to your personal or professional development? How?

List several activities in your life where you could benefit from further knowledge (e.g., skiing, selling, or parenting).

#1 _____

#2 _____

#3 _____

#4 _____

#5 _____

What sources do you have available that would support your efforts to increase your knowledge base (e.g., company library or specialty book store)?

#1 _____

#2 _____

#3 _____

#4 _____

#5 _____

It is a well-known fact that there is no correlation between formal education and success. Some of the most successful individuals in history had very little or no formal education. Thomas Edison had three months of formal education, and Abraham Lincoln was self-taught. Just because you may have a degree, doesn't mean you will be successful. I saw fellow West Point graduates who excelled academically while in school, however, once they were placed in a leadership role, they were unable to effectively communicate with peers and superiors alike. It's how you apply what you learn to meet the needs of others, that in most cases, creates success or failure, acceptance or rejection.

There is however, as Earl Nightingale noted, a direct correlation between an individual's proficiency in language and the degree of success they will achieve. Your ability to express yourself clearly, with an excellent vocabulary and correct grammar is key to your success. When someone speaks, do you generally have a sense about (idea of) their professional skills and knowledge? Your answer is probably "yes." As a result, does this influence your motivation to work, or not work, with that person or company? Your answer is likely to be "yes" again.

The average American reads less than one book a year! In fact, he or she reads the first chapter of a book, then closes it, never to be read again!

The average American learns only five new vocabulary words a year, and "awesome" doesn't count!

Effective communication provides the building blocks for successful relationships at work and at home. It's one of the major influences in the decision making process in the world of work. In a work setting, how do you react when someone responds with poor use of language? Are you as comfortable doing business with them as you were before? You may not be, especially if they continue to communicate ineffectively. It is important to invest time to continually develop your language proficiency. Every new word generates new meaning and therefore, new knowledge and growth. It's a wonderful circle of learning.

Exercise #24 - Communication/Efficiency Link

Author Tom Peters once noted in his *Speed is Life* presentation, that companies will succeed or fail based on their ability or inability to process information, i.e., communicate. If a company communicates its product or service benefits slowly and processes its business activities sluggishly, it's likely that it will be out of operation quickly. The same is true of an individual. What is your level of efficiency in your career and personal life? Are there "tools" that could help you communicate more efficiently with others (e.g., fax machine, voice mail, car telephone, enhanced computer system, or audio cassettes)?

Notes: _____

_____

_____

List several items that you or your workplace might need to help you to communicate more efficiently, and therefore, provide better service to clients.

#1 _____

#2 _____

#3 _____

#4 _____

#5 _____

Take advantage of opportunities to learn! Read books, watch educational/motivational videos, listen to audio cassettes, and attend seminars. As much as you might want to listen to your favorite music station, is it providing you that extra edge over the competition, or making you a more effective parent or manager? Would listening to an audio tape on a personal or professional interest of yours be more beneficial to your overall success?

Experience is the validation of knowledge. It provides the testing ground for what we learn. You can read all the books there are on scuba diving, but if you don't get in the water in the first place, it will be difficult to see the fish in their habitat. The steps of "Totally Forgive," "Have Self-Esteem," "Elevate Your Attitude & Enthusiasm," "Sustain Self-Control," and "Always Be Honest/Always Dream & Set Goals" all contribute to knowledge, however it is the *application* of this knowledge that is necessary for achievement.

Affirmation S - I continually improve my communication skills by increasing my vocabulary, reading more, listening to audio cassettes, and attending seminars.

Affirmation T - I conduct my business with the utmost efficiency. The speed at which I effectively communicate my product and/or service is vital my success.

Notes: _____

_____

_____

_____

_____

Step 6A: *Understand People*

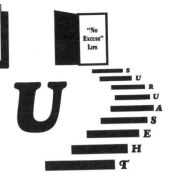

"There is a direct correlation between communication and language, and the degree of success you achieve."
— *Earl Nightingale*

*Objective T - To understand the different personalities and how communication impacts your achievement.

Everyone's different. In order to communicate effectively with others at home and at work, we need to understand the various personality types or temperments. The best way to do that is to take a genuine interest in people, discuss their dominant need, and then fill it.

One of the most effective principles of effective communication is listening; it can help us to understand the other person. Someone once said, "We were given two ears and only one month. We need to listen twice as much as we talk." When we give our undivided attention to another person, we are communicating the message that we care. When they complete their interaction with you, they are likely to feel happy about you and themselves, and believe that you have excellent communication skills. People are most interested in themselves and when you pay attention to them, they usually love it. *People don't care how much you know until they know how much you care.*

People perceive by three primary means (learning styles): visually, auditory, and kinesthetic. Visuals focus on the things they see. Sight is the dominant sense of the visual, which includes 60 percent of us. They may say, "I *see* what you mean." Auditory people are most interested in the way things sound. They might say, "I *hear* what you're saying." When a visual and an auditory get together, they'll communicate better when they understand each other's dominant sense. Kinesthetics perceive their world by how they feel. They're interested in the atmosphere of the room. Is it hot or cold? Are they pleased to be there? They may comment, "I *feel* comfortable."

All of us share a little of all three learning styles. How do you think this impacts the way we communicate?

The biggest key to effective communication is understanding the four personality types: **"D" - Dominant, "I" - Inspirational, "S" - Supportive**, and **"C" Cautious**; **DISC**. Most of us fall predominately into one area. None of the personality types are "good" or "bad" or "right" or "wrong." We are not meant to pass judgment. We are to just observe behavior so that we can better understand and deal with the person. This will help us more effectively meet their needs with our service or product.

Outgoing

Reserved

"D" - Dominant — The "D" quadrant represents a person who is both outgoing and task-oriented. The letter "D" is used because this personality type tends to be a **dominant, driving, demanding, determined, decisive, doer.** The exclamation point symbolizes this is a person with a "do-it-now" attitude. They need to be in charge. They are likely to control and tell, and dictate. Their eye contact tends to be forceful and persistent. They are usually direct. Their body movements are precise. They're in control. They often handle things well. About 10 percent of all people are "D's." Give the "D" options; it gives them a sense of control!

"I" - Inspirational — The "I" quadrant represents a person who is both outgoing and people-oriented. The letter "I" is used because this personality type tends to be **Inspirational, Influencing, Inducing, Impressive, Interactive, Interesting,** and **Interested** in people. The star symbolizes that this is a person who likes to "make-it-fun." They need to be noticed. They enjoy "show-and-tell." They are enthusiastic and talk through great hand, arm, and body movement. They smile and go on-and-on. They'll often not pay attention to you; they're thinking about something else. They like awards and rewards. About 25 to 30 percent of all people are "I's." Give "I's" recognition.

"S" - Supportive — The "S" quadrant represents a person who is both reserved and people-oriented. The letter "S" is used because this personality type tends to be a **supportive, stable, steady, sentimental, shy, status-quo, specialist.** The plus-minus sign suggests they are flexible and have a "more-or-less" attitude. They need to be accepted. They relate to the world through feelings; they are kinesthetic. They tend to show their emotions, yet aren't very assertive. They communicate how they feel through body language. They are often enjoyable and pleasant to be around. About 30 to 35 percent of all people are "S's." Accept the "S"; they need your approval!

"C"- Cautious — The "C" quadrant represents a person who is both reserved and task-oriented. The letter "C" is used to indicate a personality that tends to be **cautious, competent, calculating, concerned, careful,** and **contemplative.** The question mark symbolizes a person who asks questions because they have a need to know. They need to be accurate. They tend to ask and control. They want the facts and don't say much. They may have a "closed" personality and don't worry about much. About 20 to 25 percent of all people are "C's." Give the "C's" the facts.

Listen empathically. Look into the person's eyes so they know you care. It's not just what you hear with your ears that's important, but also what communication you receive with your eyes. Listening is a great way to show your love for others. People need someone to listen to them.

Exercise #25 - What Is Your Personality/Temperament?

Now you have had an opportunity to get a basic idea of what each personality type is like. What type do you think you are? What one or two quadrants best describe your personality? To help you figure it out, we've developed a "Personality Type Indicator."

Most people's personalities consist of a combination of characteristics, with one or two of the quadrants being most obvious. Keep in mind that this identification is meant to help you understand and accept yourself and others better. It is not to be used to label or value judge yourself and others. The more you know yourself, the better able you are to become more skillful in areas that are hindering you. You'll be better equipped to balance your traits.

There are two ways to approach determining your style. You could ask someone who knows you well to take the "Personality Type Indicator," noting the characteristics that describe you best. And, of course, you can take the Indicator yourself! When you do, be as objective and honest as possible.

Once the Indicator has been scored, you are likely to better understand why you react to people and situations as you do. I believe you'll find that it is enjoyable to share your results and give others the opportunity to take the Indicator as well.

Instructions: For each row across labelled A through Z, circle one word that best describes the way you are most of the time. Be sure to circle one word only in each lettered row. Do this for both your "Beneficial Attributes" and "Detrimental Attributes." Observe that the detrimental ones are beneficial ones taken to an extreme.

Notes: _____

_____

_____

_____

PERSONALITY TYPE INDICATOR

	ONE	TWO	THREE	FOUR
	BENEFICIAL ATTRIBUTES FROM A-Z			
A	Strong-willed	Involved	Reserved	Loyal
B	Adventurous	Talkative	Mediator	Respectful
C	Independent	Optimistic	Sentimental	Sensitive
D	Productive	Persuasive	Steady	Planner
E	Practical	Fervent	Easygoing	Idealistic
F	Resourceful	Imaginative	Calm	Deep
G	Optimistic	Outgoing	Stable	Behaved
H	Results Oriented	Cheery	Humorous	Persistent
I	Decisive	Enthusiastic	Diplomatic	Serious
J	Determined	Fun	Dependable	Competent
K	Competitive	Popular	Conservative	Orderly
L	Positive	Dramatic	Status Quo	Analytical
M	Efficient	Cute	Soft-Hearted	Thorough
N	Leader	Warm	Trustworthy	Quiet
O	Confident	Friendly	Tolerant	Self-sacrificing
P	Controlled	Playful	Single-minded	Perfectionistic
Q	Independent	Bouncy	Friendly	Considerate
R	Direct	Personable	Specialist	Compliant
S	Bold	Refreshing	Good Listener	Cultured
T	Tenacious	Carefree	Efficient	Aesthetic
U	Persuasive	Spontaneous	Systematic	Musical
V	Self-reliant	Compassionate	Sensitive	Chartmaker
W	Mover	Interested in People	Great Finisher	Gifted
X	Doer	Promoter	Cooperative	Contemplative
Y	Quick to Respond	Delightful	Helpful	Consistent
Z	Likes Challenges	Animated	Practical	Industrious
*				

* Fill-in the total number of words circled for each column.

PERSONALITY TYPE INDICATOR

DETRIMENTAL ATTRIBUTES FROM A-Z

	ONE	TWO	THREE	FOUR
A	Pushy	Undisciplined	Shy	Alienated
B	Manipulative	Overly Talkative	Conforming	Critical
C	Cruel	Egocentric	Slow	Bashful
D	Domineering	Emotional	Worrisome	Self-Centered
E	Crafty	Reacting	Stingy	Calculating
F	Self-sufficient	Directionless	Unsure	Unforgiving
G	Tactless	Loud	Indecisive	Moody
H	Tough	Sloppy	Reluctant	Revengeful
I	Sarcastic	Forgetful	Spectator	Negative
J	Angry	Undependable	Dependent	Stuffy
K	Frank	Brassy	Unenthusiastic	Easily Offended
L	Demanding	Exaggerative	Mumbles	Rigid
M	Reckless	Restless	Awkward	Resentful
N	Unaffectionate	Manipulative	Blank	Depressed
O	Argumentative	Repetitious	Selfish	Theoretical
P	Intolerant	Fearful	Timid	Impossible to Satisfy
Q	Unemotional	Permissive	Doubtful	Picky
R	Inconsiderate	Unrealistic	Plain	Impractical
S	Rash	Impulsive	Self-protective	Unsociable
T	Unsympathetic	Scatterbrained	Indifferent	Insecure
U	Workaholic	Weak-willed	Aimless	Doubtful
V	Stubborn	Show-off	Inflexible	Worrisome
W	Resistant	Unstable	Fearful	"Nosey"
X	Fighter	Interrupts	Resentful	Indecisive
Y	Impatient	Wants Credit	Easily Manipulated	Compulsive
Z	Proud	Changeable	Unmotivated	Fearful
*				

* Fill-in the total number of words circled for each column.

FINAL TOTALS: (Add your totals from Beneficial Attributes and Detrimental Attributes together.)

_____   _____   _____   _____

After you've completed your circling in both the "Beneficial" and "Detrimental" tables, add up the number of circles in each column numbered one through four for each table. Add your totals from Beneficial Attributes and Detrimental Attributes together for each column. The higher the Final Total number, the more you favor the personality type represented by that column. Column One is a **"D"** (Dominant), Column Two is an **"I"** (Inspirational), Column Three is an **"S"** (Supportive), and Column Four is a **"C"** (Cautious). If you have six or seven in each column, your personality is pretty well balanced!

For more complete information on personality types we suggest you read *Positive Personality Profiles* by Dr. Robert A. Rohm. You may obtain this book as well as get a computer analysis of your personality by contacting Personality Insights, Inc. See the "Resources" section in the back of your *No Excuse-I'm Doing It!* book.

Exercise #26 - Use of the Perception and Personality Type Information

#1 I am a visual, auditory, kinesthetic person *(circle one).*

#2 My spouse (or other important person in my life) is a visual, auditory, kinesthetic person *(circle one).*

#3 I am a   D   I   S   C   *(circle one).*   *(The column where you had the most points or the two columns if there was an equal amount of the highest point value in both columns.)*

#4 My spouse (or other important person in my life) is a   D   I   S   C   *(circle one).*

#5 I can better communicate with my spouse (or other important person in my life) by:

_____

_____

#6 I now understand the reasons _____
(someone who may have puzzled me before) behaves as they do.

#6a It is because _____

_____

#7 I want to work on the following skills so that I can develop a more balanced personality:

_____

_____

_____

#8 I want to share the three learning styles and the "Personality Type Indicator" with the following people so that we can communicate better:

_____

_____

_____

Affirmation U - I communicate with feelings. I invest time and energy to understand other people's feelings and listen empathically.

Affirmation V - I understand the three learning styles and four personality types. I communicate effectively with people.

Notes: _____

_____

_____

_____

_____

_____

_____

_____

_____

_____

_____

_____

_____

_____

Sincerity

Wear a smile.

Remember names correctly.

Find out what their interest is and talk about that.

Be a good listener.

Arouse in the person a want.

Make the other person feel important.

Avoid argument.

Don't judge people, understand them.

Admit your wrongs right away.

Begin everything in a friendly way.

Agree immediately, get a yes yes.

Don't boast about yourself.

Let people think it was their idea.

See things from the other person's view (walk a mile in their shoes).

Be sympathetic about other views that differ.

Dramatize your ideas.

Throw down a challenge.

Begin with compliments, before you straighten them out.

Talk about your mistakes before correcting someone.

Ask questions and make suggestions, don't order.

Let the other person save face.

Recognize the slightest improvement and every improvement.

Give the person a good reputation to live up to.

Encourage people, make their faults seem easy to correct.

Make people happy about the things that you suggest.

Author Unknown

Step 7: *Remember to Honor Family & Friends*

"The best portion of a good man's life - his little nameless, unremembered acts of kindness and love."
— *William Wordsworth*

*Objective U - **To understand that honoring family and friends is reflected in your successes and failures.**

*Objective V - **To build your personal tree of family and friends.**

As you begin to approach the top of the *Staircase,* take time to give yourself some positive recognition for your efforts. You have been given the opportunity to accomplish many wonderful things. However, this next step is extremely important to achieving real fulfillment. A house without caring inhabitants, no matter how big and beautiful, is not a home. Remembering family and friends are the "s's" in success; the beginning and the end.

The legacy we leave to our family and friends will be the definition of our achievements in life, and the purest description of our success. How many times during our run along the *Staircase-of-Success* do we forget and take for granted those in our lives who are most important? It's what we give to them that will reap the greatest rewards and it's what we take for granted that can result in the greatest losses.

I would like to share with you a personal story that I feel illustrates this special step along our *Staircase.* One of my early speaking engagements was at Union College in Schenectady, N.Y., and I was asked to present our program to approximately 90 sorority sisters. That was a difficult invitation to decline! I felt that since my daughter Nicole, age seven at the time, had never heard me present before, this would be an appropriate setting. When I had concluded my presentation and we were driving home, Nicole turned to me and said, "Dad, don't stop what your doing. It seems to help a lot of people." You can't put a price tag on the kind words of a child, but if I could, all the money in the world could not substitute for the happiness I felt inside at that moment. To see your child feeling and valuing what you do is a magical moment.

In most cases, it's never too late to give to those who have given to you, whether they are living under the same roof with you or not. The closer your relationship, the more they are a reflection of you, your strengths and weaknesses. Visualize for a minute that we are all trees. Some of us are oak trees, some are maple, and some are balsam trees. It is our branches that represent our health and beauty, much like our family and friends do. If one main branch dies the tree will survive; if four or five main branches die, the tree eventually dies.

Exercise #27 - Our Tree House

Who are the most important people in your life? Recently, how have you shown your appreciation for those you love? Do they know it? Our daily lives, as alluded to in "Sustain Self-Control", may take a tremendous amount of energy and time away from our family. However, our career is not to be used as an excuse to neglect those we love. The importance you place on anything or anyone determines your level of effort towards it. When you place more importance on your family and friends, it's likely you'll want to spend more time with them.

Create your own tree of family and friends. List those who you enjoy and relate to the most.

#1 _____

#2 _____

#3 _____

#4 _____

#5 _____

#6 _____

#7 _____

#8 _____

#9 _____

#10 _____

As a result of the closeness we may share with many of our family and friends, emotion, rather than practical thinking, may tend to prevail. Why? They are aware of many of our personality characteristics and traits that we would rather forget or deny (e.g., anger and ineffective habits). Our family and friends tend to be the most truthful with us, and as a result, may touch certain emotional nerve centers. It can be this emotion that frequently causes the communication breakdown between ourselves and our family. How you feel about yourself will determine how well you accept their honesty and criticism. Whether they are correct or incorrect, they do it because, in some way, they care. Once you accept yourself and your own imperfect behavior, you will find it much easier to appreciate, respect, and accept those who are closest to you.

How can we show our appreciation for those who have given of themselves to us? Letters, cards, or a phone call are just a few of the ways we can show our gratitude. Have you ever thought of writing a letter to your parents or someone close to you, expressing your appreciation for them and their influence in your life? In many cases it would be the nicest gift they had ever received from you.

Make a commitment to select two very special people to you, and show them, in your own way, that you appreciate their friendship and love.

#1 _____

#2 _____

Remember those in your life who have given of themselves to you. The bonds formed with those loved ones are bonds that may last a lifetime.

Affirmation W- I honor the most important people in my life, my family and friends, for they are always part of my achievements.

Affirmation X - I sincerely appreciate my family and friends, and make every effort to demonstrate this gratitude to them.

Notes: _____

_____

_____

_____

_____

_____

_____

_____

_____

_____

Step 8: *Upraise Your Determination*

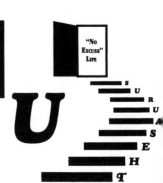

"All our dreams can come true — if we have the courage to pursue them."

— *Walt Disney*

*Objective W - **To understand that success takes the determination to keep going, even when faced with what you perceive to be insurmountable odds.**

*Objective X - **To construct your puzzle of success, and to develop the desire to see all your dreams come true.**

As you begin to incorporate the many principles of the *THESAURUS Factor* into your life, you may be faced with many obstacles and challenges that may influence your progress. Determination is that one special ingredient that can prevent you from returning to an existence of mediocrity. Desire is the reason for upraised determination, for without desire, there is little reason to employ any of the previously discussed principles. Be determined to achieve your goals and dreams, knowing that these accomplishments will benefit you and others around you.

Have you ever quit? Did you ever regret that decision? Was there ever a moment that you wanted to quit? Have you ever decided not to quit, and felt great about the decision?

It's human nature to either fight or flee when faced with difficult challenges. Your ability to see things through even when times are tough is a rare attribute. It's much easier to quit and move-on to something else when your job, your family, and other parts of your life do not seem to be going your way. It takes a great deal more courage and strength to accept life's challenges and to see the opportunities available. One of the shortest recorded commencement speeches in history was given by Winston Churchill during WWII. He stood in front of the graduating class and said, "There is only one thing I would like to say to you, and that is never give in! Never give in! Never, never, never, never .... In nothing great or small, large or petty, never give in except to convictions of honor and good sense!" I am sure that the members of the graduating class always remembered that short and powerful speech.

As an entrepreneur, there have been many times that I wanted to throw-in-the-towel, but something inside gave me the courage to keep trying. I realized that if I truly loved what I was doing, then every attempt to make it work was worth the hardship and frustration. If you truly love what you do, and believe in your abilities and talents, then the word "quit" can be eliminated from your vocabulary.

Exercise #28 - Quitting Versus Change

Quitting is often a result of finding an excuse for not continuing (e.g., too hard, not enough time or money, or can't communicate). Quitting is usually falsely justified by the excuses we conjure up in our minds. It may be much easier to "justify" quitting than it is to finish or accomplish a difficult challenge. When you intensely want something you know can make a positive difference in your life and the lives of others, you would be best not to quit. Can you imagine if Neil Armstrong, in the middle of his space training, said to himself, "This will be one small step for man, but I'm not taking it because I am too scared and it will take too much hard work"? What if Martin Luther King Jr., in the middle of his *I Have A Dream* speech, said, "I think I better stop now, I don't want to get hurt or cause any more problems"? The things in your life that you want the most, and feel are the most important, are often the most difficult to achieve and have the greatest risk.

Change is a result of the conflict between risk and desire. If your desire outweighs the risk, yet you change your mind, that is quitting. If risk outweighs your desire, then a change may be appropriate. Only you in your heart can make those decisions. Change can result after weighing the positive and negative in a situation, analyzing, making a decision, and exhausting all other options. You need to always ask yourself, "What is the reason for this change?" Is the grass greener on the other side of the fence? Am I changing because of opportunity, or because of difficulty? Successful people welcome difficulty and challenges, because it allows them to experience, grow, and in most cases, achieve in areas that few others do. Always remember the story of the book *The Little Engine That Could.*

Are there any areas in your life where you feel, if you had worked at it a little harder or a little longer, the situation would have turned out the way you wanted it?

#1 _____

#2 _____

#3 _____

#4 _____

#5 _____

What changes have you made that have been positive as a result of your evaluation of your situation?

#1 _____

#2 _____

#3 _____

#4 _____

#5 _____

What challenges are you faced with today that you have a strong desire to overcome but there are many difficulties (e.g., starting a new business or a new relationship)?

#1 _____

#2 _____

#3 _____

#4 _____

#5 _____

Remember, the past decisions about which you have just reflected have come and gone. If any have resulted in regrets, let go of this excess baggage now. The flow of success is circular, and all principles interact for the support of others. Regrets are not to be used as an excuse for future failure. Forgiving yourself will help!

Exercise #29 - The Puzzle of Life

Life is multifaceted. There may be many areas in life that you want to experience, and many aspects of your life that you would like to see fulfilled. You may dream of love, success, money, peace, happiness, harmony, health, spiritual fulfillment, and more. Whatever your dreams are, you can make them come true!

Our lives are very much like jigsaw puzzles. Imagine your life a 1000 piece jigsaw puzzle of a beautiful landscape. You open the box, dump the pieces on a table, and you are "born." As your life goes, so does the puzzle, piece by piece. Some fit easily, many fit with more difficulty, and some you make fit. To see the whole picture, all pieces need to come together. At first, we put the frame of the puzzle together, then the easy parts, such as those with distinct shapes and colors. Early in life, in most cases, we learn to walk, talk, and make basic decisions.

However, we reach a point in the puzzle, as with life, that of those 1000 pieces, we have 465 left to place; and of the beautiful landscape all that is left is blue sky. We look at the puzzle, as with our lives, and ask ourselves, "How am I ever going to get the rest of my puzzle (life) together?" The key is to always keep trying to put the pieces together. As a puzzle is incomplete with missing pieces, so is life. Always strive to complete the puzzle, always strive to complete your life. When all the pieces finally fit together, in one or more areas of your life, you can then begin to see a picture of achievement.

What pieces are still left out in your puzzle (e.g., further education, more effort in your career or business, more family time, better health)?

#1 _____

#2 _____

#3 _____

#4 _____

#5 _____

"There is no success without challenges."

Your greatest rewards in life will be the result of your greatest efforts. Your home of success is ready for the finishing touches as you approach the last step on *Staircase-of-Success.*

Affirmation Y - I accept all of life's challenges and have the determination to succeed at all my endeavors.

Affirmation Z - I possess the courage and strength to fulfill all of my dreams, and have the self-discipline to always keep working on achieving my goals and dreams.

Notes: _____

_____

_____

Step 9: *Succeed & Balance Your Life*

"Make the most of yourself, for that is all there is of you."
— Ralph Waldo Emerson

*Objective Y- **To understand the working relationship between the principles of *THESAURUS*.**

*Objective Z- **To conclude that happiness and fulfillment with your personal and professional life can be achieved by adopting a philosophy of self-responsibility and living a "No Excuse!" lifestyle.**

Congratulations on reaching the top of your staircase.

It's now time to integrate your unique talents and experiences with the principles of "No Excuse!" Your "home of success" which you just had an opportunity to build is likely to be ready to move into. How does it look? "Succeed & Balance Your Life" is the implementation of the principles of *THESAURUS* into your personal and professional life. You'll discover, that by adopting a philosophy of self-responsibility, integrity, and purpose and incorporating the principles of *THESAURUS,* happiness and fulfillment will come much easier.

The foundation of your home; self-responsibility, integrity, and defining purpose and success are the cornerstones of your fulfillment. Without them, you will have very little direction or meaning for living. Your actions can support your purpose every day, because your purpose gives you a reason for using your special talents.

The principles of *THESAURUS* provide the means to maintain focus and direction in your life. Once you employ "Totally Forgive" in your life, you can let go of using yourself, others, or the environment, as an excuse for failure. As a result, you immediately begin to practice the philosophy of self-responsibility.

When you do forgive, a wonderful feeling of self-esteem begins to emanate. How could you not feel happy with yourself when you are honest and sincere with people, and give of yourself to others? You will discover that you can only be at your best for others when you are at your best for yourself.

Having self-esteem helps you have the self-confidence and belief in yourself to work to achieve whatever you set your mind to. Only with self-esteem will you truly be able to appreciate yourself and others.

You "Elevate Your Attitude & Enthusiasm" as a result of enhanced self-esteem. This sets the tone for your perception about life and how you deal with life. Your attitude and enthusiasm are two of the most powerful influences on both yourself and other people. The ability to be optimistic and turn negative situations into positive ones is a skill more people need to develop. It takes energy to commit to it. It's worth the effort. You can develop into a "magnet" who attracts other optimistic and enthusiastic people.

Your ability to "Sustain Self-Control" is the measure of your patience and professionalism; and is a reflection of your ability to forgive, your self-esteem, and your attitude towards yourself and others. Self-control is one of the critical elements in maintaining consistency on your journey to success. Recall that you can do 100 positive things, but it only takes one blunder to set you back many steps.

"Always Be Honest" is a principle to always uphold. It is a principle, that when jeopardized, can result in disaster. Your adherence to honesty can help propel you forward towards success more quickly.

"Always Dream & Set Goals" is your definition of success. It is the one principle that all others contribute to. Without dreams and goals, you have no direction and no definition of success. They can help you to motivate yourself. With strong dreams and goals, you can do almost anything. When you put your heart and soul into something you love and truly want, getting there is half the fun.

When you "Upgrade Your Knowledge," you get the key to the doors of success. The achievement of goals is the result of incorporating the principles of success. Knowledge provides the means to learn *how* to incorporate them. Knowledge is the refueling mechanism for continued achievement. The more you refuel, the further you can go.

How you "Remember to Honor Family & Friends" will help to determine how successful you become. What you give to them, and the legacy you leave behind for them, will be the results of your achievements and failures. Part of you always lives on when you are remembered for the love and kindness that you gave to your family and friends.

Your belief in yourself and your commitment to a better world will support your "Upraised Determination" to achieve greatness in your life. You have the talent and now the principles to make your dreams come true, and receive the best of what life has to offer.

Remember, the difficult thing about life is not so much the challenges with the external, rather, it is the challenges with the internal. When you utilize the principles outlined in this program, you can "Succeed & Balance Your Life" and you'll be more likely to view the challenges you face as opportunities, not disappointments.

Always remember that someone else's success is never greater than your own. Their success may not be the type of success that fulfills your dreams and brings about happiness for you. Your happiness is unique, how you overcome your excuses is unique, and what you need to forgive is unique. If we base our success on a scale structured by others we "open the gate" for a flood of excuses to control our lives. Excuses others use may influence our perceptions of success and our ability to attain it. Your definitions of purpose and success, your integrity, and your implementation of self-responsibility can help you create the success you want for your life.

Always remember this: "It's easy to make a dollar, but it's more important to make a difference." You possess the gifts to make a difference in your life and the lives of others. "No Excuse!" can assist you in the achievement of that goal.

One of my favorite quotes of all time is by *Ralph Waldo Emerson* on his definition of success:

> *To laugh often and much; to win the respect of intelligent people and the*
> *affection of children; to earn the appreciation of honest critics and endure*
> *the betrayal of false friends; to appreciate beauty, to find the best in others;*

to leave the world a bit better, whether by a healthy child, a garden patch or a redeemed social condition; to know even one life has breathed easier because you have lived. This is to have succeeded.

Affirmation AA - I now have the necessary attributes to achieve all my goals and dreams.

Affirmation BB - I always strive to live a life of self-responsibility; a "No Excuse" life.

I congratulate you once again on what you have achieved and I truly wish you unlimited success in all your endeavors.

There truly is "No Excuse" not to be successful in your life.

Notes _____

_____

_____

_____

_____

_____

_____

_____

_____

_____

_____

_____

_____

_____